EARLY AMERICAN FAMILY

Meet the Webbers
of Philadelphia

by John J. Loeper

BENCHMARK BOOKS

MARSHALL CAVENDISH
NEW YORK

Benchmark Books
Marshall Cavendish Corporation
99 White Plains Road
Tarrytown, New York 10591-9001

Illustrations by James Watling
Musical score and arrangement by Jerry Silverman
Map by Rodica Prato
Photo research by Matthew J. Dudley
The photographs in this book are used by permission and through the courtesy of:
The Historical Society of Pennsylvania: 1, 26. *Archive Photos*: 12, 46 (left & right).
The Image Bank: Joanna McCarthy, 17; G.K.&Vicky Hart, 19; Steve Niedorf, back
cover. © 1998 Rod Berry: 27, 29, 34. *The Library Company of Philadelphia*: 36, 41.
Baker Library, Harvard Business School: 45. *Corbis-Bettmann*: 49. © *Wiliam B. Fol-
som 1998*: 51. *Unicorn Stock Photos/Charlie Schmidt*: 55. © *Jerry Millovoi*: 59.

Library of Congress Cataloging-in-Publication Data
Loeper, John J.
Meet the Webbers of Philadelphia / John J. Loeper
p.   cm.— (Early American family)
Includes bibliographical references and index.
Summary: Chronicles the history of a free black family in Philadelphia during the
eighteenth and nineteenth centuries, focusing on Amos Webber who became a
musician, property owner, and abolitionist.
ISBN 0-7614-0843-6 (lib. bdg.)
1. Free Afro-Americans—Pennsylvania—Philadelphia Region—Social life and
customs—Juvenile literature. 2. Free Afro-Americans—Pennsylvania—
Philadelphia Region—Biography—Juvenile literature. 3. Philadelphia (Pa.)—
Social life and customs—Juvenile literarature. 4. Webber family—Juvenile
literature. 5. Philadelphia (Pa.)—Social life and customs. [1. Webber family.
2. Afro-Americans—Biography.] I. Title. II. Series: Loeper, John J.
Early American family.
F158.9.N4L64 1999   974.8'1100496073—DC21   97-42200   CIP   AC

Printed in Hong Kong
1 3 5 6 4 2

To the Reader

Blacks have lived in America since its beginnings. They played an important part in the birth and the growth of our nation. Some were free; most were not.

Before President Abraham Lincoln took his oath of office in March 1861, seven Southern states had withdrawn from the Union. They set up a rival government and seized United States property within their borders. This was the most serious matter any president had ever faced, and it led to what is known as the Civil War. Hundreds of books have been written attempting to explain its causes. Most historians agree that the dispute revolved around the enslavement of blacks.

Slavery is an ancient practice and was once part of American life. The first Africans arrived in Virginia at the Jamestown colony aboard a Dutch warship in 1619. They were indentured servants, bound to work for a certain number of years to satisfy their debts. By 1700, large numbers of Africans had been brought to America in chains and sold as slaves. These people became the property of their owners. By 1760, almost all of the blacks in colonial America were enslaved. Slavery was especially common in the South, where large plantations relied on cheap labor.

Although slavery thrived, some blacks were still free. Most of them lived in the North. Some free blacks were former indentured servants; some had bought their freedom or had been freed by their owners; others were runaways.

Pennsylvania was a stronghold of free blacks. This was due to the Quaker opposition to slavery. As early as 1775 the Society of Friends had established an antislavery society and welcomed former slaves to Pennsylvania. Most of them settled in or near the city of Philadelphia. A number of free black families lived outside Philadelphia in the village of Attleborough, in Bucks County. They governed themselves, built their own churches, and operated their own businesses.

This is the story of one of those families. It is based on the diaries of Amos Webber, which were only recently discovered in the Baker Library of the Harvard Business School. They paint a vivid picture of the everyday life of black Americans in the mid-nineteenth century.

Let's go now to Pennsylvania and meet the Webbers.

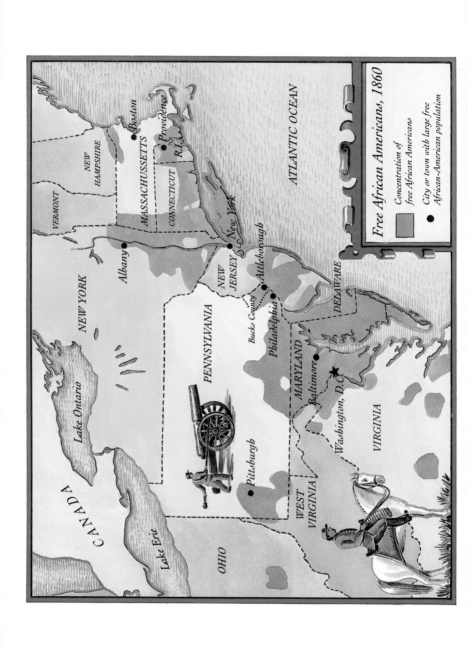

Free African Americans, 1860

Concentration of
free African Americans

City or town with large free
African-American population

ATLANTIC OCEAN

CANADA

Lake Ontario

Lake Erie

NEW HAMPSHIRE

VERMONT

MASSACHUSSETTS

CONNECTICUT

R.I.

Boston

Providence

NEW YORK

Albany

New York

Attleborough

NEW JERSEY

Bucks County

Philadelphia

PENNSYLVANIA

Pittsburgh

DELAWARE

MARYLAND

Baltimore

Washington, D.C.

WEST VIRGINIA

OHIO

VIRGINIA

*T*en-year-old Amos Webber watched a wagon drawn by two gray horses as it rumbled over the cobblestones of Philadelphia. It was piled high with fresh produce on its way to the City Market.

Amos had come to the city with his older brother, Sammy. The family rented a stall in the market. His father had run it until his death in 1825. After that, his mother and brother had continued the business. They sold fruit and vegetables grown in their backyard.

The City Market's long brick arcade took up nearly half a mile along High Street, the city's main thoroughfare. This was Amos's first time in Philadelphia. Ordinarily, he stayed behind in Attleborough with his mother when Sammy

Ten-year-old Amos Webber watched a wagon drawn by two
gray horses as it rumbled over the cobblestones of Philadelphia.

went to market. But last week his mother, Fannie, had announced that he was old enough to help.

"You can clean the vegetables and wash the fruit," she had told him. "And if you are careful and polite, a customer may give you an extra penny."

It was exciting to be in the city. There was lots to see—people bustled here and there, some talking excitedly, others dashing across the street to avoid the horse-drawn carriages as they clip-clopped by. And there was music too. Musicians plucked the strings of a banjo or bowed away at a fiddle, hoping that passersby pausing to listen would feel inclined to give them a penny or two for a tune well played. An old black woman stood on a corner singing spirituals. The city vibrated with a wonderful mixture of noise and notes.

Amos loved music. His mother played the melodeon, a small reed organ. She had taught Amos how to read music and to pick out notes on the keyboard. He had already mastered several chords and was able to play a few melodies.

It was exciting to be in the city. There was lots to see.

"One day soon I will take you to a concert in Philadelphia," his mother had promised.

At that time, Philadelphia was the greatest city in America. It had a booming economy and was the cultural center of the new country. It was a jumble of shops, taverns, and amusements. The city boasted a circus, several theaters, and a number of concert halls. Many of its residents were men and women of wealth and learning. A

Philadelphia had a booming economy and was the cultural center of the new country.

writer of the time noted that "no other city is so rich, so fashionable, and so entertaining."

On his first visit, Amos fell in love with the city. He promised himself that, one day, he would live in Philadelphia and become a famous musician.

The village of Attleborough, where Amos lived with his mother and brother, lay about twenty miles northeast of Philadelphia. It had about eighty houses, a handful of shops, and several churches. Most of its 264 residents were free blacks.

Freedom for African Americans was obtained in a number of ways. Some slaves were freed by an act of legislation when the state of Pennsylvania abolished slavery in 1780. Others gained freedom through a provision in their owners' wills. A slave owner might specify as a last request that certain of his slaves or all of them be set free. More fortunate slaves purchased their freedom, but this was rare, because slaves had difficulty accumulating money. Yet some managed to do it.

This is not to say that freedom for blacks was

universally accepted—quite the contrary. Many whites objected and did so very openly. Moreover, a new idea about the master-slave relationship was developing. It was called paternalism and preached that blacks were inferior and needed a "father" to look after them. On their own, some whites said, blacks would face disaster. One white Southerner of the period wrote:

Free negroes are an intolerable nuisance that blight every neighborhood in which they live—North and South. A free negro! Why the very term seems an absurdity! Free negroes corrupt our slaves and make them less content with their situation.

John Calhoun, the leading Southern politician in Congress, saw slavery as a "positive good." "In all instances," he declared, "in which the Northern states abolished slavery, the condition of the African, instead of being improved, became worse. Free blacks invariably sink into vice and pauperism."

But the black community of Attleborough proved them wrong. True, many families were poor. But the streets and houses were well kept, and the churches were heavily attended. Being free was not a handicap.

Samuel and Fannie Webber, Amos's parents, had inherited their freedom. They were born in Philadelphia and moved to Attleborough after their marriage. Amos's grandparents on both sides had gained their freedom through a last will and testament. His mother kept her parents' discharge in a metal box under her bed. It read:

> I, Joseph Elkton, of Northampton County in Virginia, set my hand hereunto that Thomas, a negro, and his wife Sally, a negro, shall be discharged from servitude, their children and heirs forever.

Samuel Webber had similar papers from his family. It was important to keep these documents in a safe place. A free black person's existence, even in the North, was uncertain. A white person could claim, however falsely, that the free black person was his slave. The burden of proof always rested on the accused. Then, too, a free black person might be kidnapped and brought to a Southern state, where the rights of African

Americans were severely limited. All Southern states required free blacks to carry passes and certificates of freedom. Several Southern states compelled free blacks to have assigned white guardians. Thus, free blacks everywhere—even those whose families had been free for generations—lived in constant fear of losing their freedom.

In 1846, when Amos was twenty years old, he took the first step toward realizing his dream. He moved to Philadelphia, where he found employment as a live-in servant and handyman in the household of Charles S. Wurts, a wealthy white merchant. Amos had grown into a handsome young man, trim and muscular. He smiled easily and had an outgoing personality. But Amos had a serious side. He loved music and dreamed of a musical career. His years of practice had paid off. He was an accomplished musician. Until an opportunity came along, though, he would have to find another job.

"Life here is Christian," Mr. Wurts told Amos. "Every morning and evening we all gather in the

"Life here is Christian," Mr. Wurts told Amos.

front parlor for prayer. And on the Sabbath there are no visitors allowed, and there is no cooking."

Mr. Wurts, who was deeply religious, served on the board of the Sunday School Union, a group that encouraged young people to study the Bible.

Amos had no difficulty with his employer's demands. He had been an active member of the Colored Methodist Society in Attleborough and had attended the church school. He had learned to read and write there. Mr. Wurts often asked Amos to read aloud passages from the Bible during prayer time.

Amos found the city's black life much different from that of Attleborough. Although most of Philadelphia's blacks were poor, there was little deliberate segregation. Blacks lived in all of the city's twenty-four districts. Blacks could attend theaters and concert halls. And there were several prominent black Philadelphians, like Stephen Smith, James Forten, Robert Purvis, and Jacob White, who were wealthy and respected citizens. It was a comfortable and civilized city with numerous black churches. These offered the black population a variety of social activities, and Amos joined in.

"I'm told that you play the piano," Reverend Benjamin Templeton, pastor of the Second African Presbyterian Church, said to Amos one Sunday after the morning service.

"Yes, and I play the violin too," said Amos. "My mother was a strict teacher."

"Yes, and I play the violin too. My mother was a strict teacher. She insisted that I practice every day. Thanks to her I can play the piano, the violin, and the organ. I practiced on the organ at our church in Attleborough."

"Would you be willing to play for one of our social gatherings?" the pastor asked. "We are having a church supper next Tuesday, and piano music would add to everyone's enjoyment."

"I would be pleased to play," Amos replied.

The following Tuesday evening, Amos played for the church social. He chose some light classical pieces and a popular song, "Home, Sweet Home."

An exile from home, splendor dazzles in vain,
Oh, give me my lowly thatched cottage again;
The birds singing gaily, that come at my call;
Give me them, with that peace of mind, dearer
   than all.

Chorus

To thee, I'll return, overburdened with care,
The heart's dearest solace will smile on me there.
No more from that cottage again will I roam,
Be it ever so humble, there's no place like home.

Chorus

Everyone seemed to enjoy the piano music, especially an attractive young woman who was sitting up front. Amos noticed her when he first sat down to play. Small and dainty, she wore her hair pulled back in a bun. She smiled throughout the evening and joined in the singing with gusto.

At the end of the supper, the young woman approached him. "I like your playing," she said. "You may just be our next Francis Johnson!"

Amos was both flattered and embarrassed by her attention.

"Thank you," he replied. "I'm not that good, but I keep trying."

He looked into her bright, brown eyes and knew at once that she was someone special.

Francis Johnson was a well-known black composer and orchestra leader. He had just returned to Philadelphia following a tour of English cities, where his concerts had been enthusiastically applauded. To be compared with Francis Johnson was a high compliment.

"Most pianists play cornfield ditties," she told Amos. "It's a pleasure to hear good music."

"I owe it all to my mother," Amos explained. "She loves classical music, especially Mozart. She once took me to a Johnson concert."

The young woman smiled. "My name is Lizzie Douglass. What's yours?"

"I'm Amos Webber, famous musician," he answered.

They laughed. "You'll be famous—I just know it," she assured him.

From that time on, he and Lizzie saw a lot of each other: Amos had fallen in love. Lizzie was always on his mind, and the two spent as much time as they could with each other. They went to concerts, visited the zoo, and took long walks in Philadelphia's Fairmount Park. They talked together about music and shared their hopes and dreams with each other. Within a year, Amos proposed. Lizzie accepted and began to plan their wedding. Meanwhile, Amos searched for a better-paying job, which he found with Hart, Montgomery and Company as a handyman. The company manufactured and sold quality wallpapers.

Amos and Lizzie talked with Reverend Templeton and set a date for their wedding. It had to be a simple ceremony because there was little money to spare. The one thing they insisted on was organ music. "Our marriage must begin with music," Amos told Lizzie.

"It is not how big the wedding is, but how successful the marriage," Reverend Templeton advised. He married Amos and Lizzie on March 24, 1852.

In the early years of their married life, Amos and Lizzie rented a tiny house on Ivy Street, which they soon turned into a comfortable

Amos looked into her bright, brown eyes and knew at once that she was someone special.

home. Before long, Lizzie gave birth to a baby boy, whom they named Harry.

Because he could read and write and proved dependable, Amos became a valued employee at Hart, Montgomery. Both his salary and his responsibilities increased. Amos was put in charge of inventory. He kept track of the various wallpaper patterns and saw to it that they were always in stock. Each year his efforts were rewarded by a small increase in salary. Within a few years Amos had saved enough money to buy a house for his family. He paid four hundred

Amos became a valued employee at Hart, Montgomery.

Amos paid four hundred dollars for a small wooden house with a fireplace and a big backyard on Anita Street.

dollars for a small wooden house with a fireplace and a big backyard on Anita Street. It was in a good section of the city, and most of his neighbors were friendly. There was even enough money left over to buy a piano.

The Webbers were happy in their new home, and Lizzie urged Amos to pursue his music. Most evenings, after supper, Lizzie and little Harry sat listening to Amos playing the piano.

"Someday you will be on stage," Lizzie told him. "And folks will applaud you."

Amos smiled at his wife. He was content just to have a home, a family, and a good job.

However simple their house, the very ownership of property set Amos and Lizzie apart from their neighbors, both black and white. At the time, most Philadelphians did not own their homes. Although Amos's position at Hart, Montgomery was modest, he had steady work and a fair salary. The house on Anita Street and their other personal property placed the Webbers in the ranks of the middle class.

However, Lizzie preserved their heritage in her kitchen. Her fried fish and gumbo reminded Amos of the food he had eaten as a child in Attleborough. When Amos and Lizzie took little Harry to visit his grandmother, she often served them a heaping platter of fried fish.

"A body can't have too much fried fish," she would chuckle as she replenished their plates.

Amos's favorite meal was Sunday dinner after church, when Lizzie served her family baked ham and black-eyed peas. Her sweet potato pone was a special treat. To make the pone, Lizzie combined in a bowl:

>4 cups of shredded, raw sweet potato
>1 cup of water
>1/2 cup of brown sugar
>1/2 teaspoon of salt
>1/4 teaspoon of ground ginger

Then she placed the mixture in a casserole, dotted the top with 2 tablespoons of butter, and placed the casserole in a hot oven until the potatoes were fork-tender.

However simple their house, the very ownership of property set Amos and Lizzie apart from their neighbors.

"I think I will write a song about your pone," Amos teased her. "I will call it Pone, Sweet Pone!"

Along with his work, his home, and his music Amos Webber had another abiding interest. He was deeply concerned about the denial of civil rights to black Americans.

Although Pennsylvania had outlawed slavery in 1780, at a convention held in 1837 the state withheld from blacks the right to vote. The amendment to the state constitution concluded that blacks never had the same rights as free men and that the "African race is a degraded caste of inferior rank in society."

During the first half of the nineteenth century, blacks steadily lost their civil rights. In 1800 they were able to vote almost everywhere, but by 1855 voting by blacks was severely restricted not only in the South but in several Northern states as well. Little by little, their citizenship was eroded. As a result, free African Americans were among the most enthusiastic supporters of the growing antislavery movement. They formed antislavery societies and joined forces with white abolitionists. Together they sought an end to the enslavement of blacks. The abolition of slavery and the denial of civil rights to blacks were topics of heated discussion.

One Sunday morning, a black Presbyterian minister shouted to his congregation: "We will preach the Declaration of Independence until it is put into practice!"

Amos and Lizzie felt a heavy responsibility. Their rights as free blacks may have been restricted, but their enslaved brothers and sisters had no rights at all. Much of their antislavery activity was sponsored by the black churches. Along with Philadelphia's white abolitionists, they wrote letters to politicians, participated in protest marches and demonstrations, and helped runaway slaves. Black and white church members alike worked in the Underground Railroad, the route used by runaway slaves escaping from the South to the North that often ended in Canada. Men and women helped the fugitives along, giving them shelter and guiding them to the next place of safety. A fugitive might hide in a safe barn during the day, slip through the

Men and women helped the fugitives along, giving them shelter and guiding them to the next place of safety.

woods and fields at night, then crawl into an attic or a closet at daybreak.

In addition to his involvement with his church's antislavery activities, Amos became its organist in 1860. And Lizzie helped in the Sunday school.

Despite Philadelphia's free public education, black children were often denied access to

Amos became the organist of his church in 1860.

its schools. Black churches did what they could to help, teaching the children regular school subjects along with Bible studies in their Sunday schools. Lizzie often brought little Harry along while she taught her pupils reading, writing, and grammar.

Lizzie read the class a poem she had composed. It summed up her beliefs:

I must practice love for all,
Black or white, great or small.
I must never lie or steal,
And keep in mind how others feel.
I must not hurt, not but a fly,
For it can feel as well as I.
And with the Bible I believe,
It is better to give than to receive.

The church was located next to one of the city's many parks. On pleasant afternoons after Sunday school, Amos and Lizzie took Harry there to play. They sat on a park bench and watched the boys play tag and the girls play hopscotch. Hopscotch was a favorite pastime. Lizzie remembered playing it when she was a girl. Squares were scratched, or "scotched," onto the ground and small stones were tossed into each square. Players had to hop from one square

Next to the church (shown here) *was located one of the city's main parks.*

to another, picking up stones as they went.

While they watched, Amos began slapping his knee in rhythm with the girls' jumping.

"You can't hold the music inside of you," Lizzie told him. "It just spills out!"

"I wish music were a bigger part of my life," Amos said. "I know that I play in church and at home, but I would like to try something else. I'd like to play in a theater."

"You certainly have the talent," Lizzie replied. "Your day will come, just you wait and see."

The day Lizzie foresaw arrived one cold November evening in 1856. At a church concert in Philadelphia, Amos accompanied Elizabeth Taylor Greenfield on the piano.

Elizabeth Greenfield had been born a slave in Mississippi. When she was very young, the woman who owned her moved to Philadelphia and took Elizabeth with her. She educated her and gave her lessons in music and voice. When she was grown, Elizabeth became a concert singer. In 1851 she toured the northeastern states, giving concerts in Albany, Buffalo, Worcester, and Boston. She was compared with

*Amos and Lizzie sat on a park bench and watched the boys play
tag and the girls play hopscotch.*

Jenny Lind, a famous white singer, and a Boston newspaper described her voice as "astonishing" and "remarkable." A tour of European cities followed with equal success. Her beauty and her voice led people to call her the Black Swan.

When Elizabeth Greenfield was asked to give a concert for the Chilo Church, she agreed, but insisted on having an accomplished pianist accompany her. The pastor suggested Amos Webber, and he auditioned for the job. Greenfield loved his playing and hired him on the spot. At the end of the concert, the audience gave her a standing ovation. Graciously, she turned and motioned to Amos. He stood and took a bow. The audience went wild! They had loved his playing as much as Elizabeth Greenfield's singing.

The next morning the Philadelphia newspapers reviewed the concert. One reporter wrote: "Amos Webber's playing was extraordinary. He has complete control of the keyboard."

"Did you hear that, Amos," Lizzie exclaimed across the breakfast table. "The man says you are extraordinary!"

Elizabeth Greenfield's beauty and her voice led people to call her the Black Swan.

At the end of the concert, the audience gave Elizabeth Greenfield a standing ovation. Graciously, she turned and motioned to Amos.

"Ex-ord-nary," little Harry repeated after his mother.

"I could have told him that," Lizzie continued. "My extraordinary husband, Amos Webber, the famous pianist!"

A wide smile crossed Amos Webber's face. His childhood dreams had come true. He lived in Philadelphia and had become a recognized musician.

But sad days were just around the corner for Amos and Lizzie. On December 23, 1859, their son Harry died. He had caught a cold, and his fever could not be controlled. His death certificate said that little Harry died of "an inflammation of the brain." His funeral was two days later, on Christmas Day. He was five years and four months old. Amos and Lizzie were grief-stricken. With Harry's death, all the music in Amos drained away. The joy of their lives was gone.

As time passed, both Amos and Lizzie devoted themselves more and more to the abolitionist movement. Amos worked with such prominent blacks as Harriet Tubman and Frederick Douglass, raising money and attending

May 1858

Thermometer 7 O'clock A.M.; 3 O'clock P.M.

Week day	deg	Wind	Weather	deg	Wind	Weather
Satu 1	58	NE	Clear	73	NE	Clear
Sun 2	—	NE	Cloudy	—	NE	Cloudy
Mon 3	51	NW	Clear	59	SE	Clear
Tues 4	50	SE	Cloudy day	61	SE	Raining	majority
Wed 5	56	SE	Cloudy. Election	61	SE	Raining	Elliott mayor 4072
Thurs 6	56	SE	Cloudy	63	SE	Clear = Alexander Henry
Frid 7	58	NE	Raining	61	NE	Cloudy
Sat 8	59	NE	Cloudy	63	NE	Clear
Sun 9	—	SE	Cloudy	—	SE	Hazzy	and then shot himself
Mon 10	57	S	Raining	64	W	Cloudy	in Franklin square
Tues 11	58	NE	Raining	62	SE	Raining	woman this morning
Wed 12	55	NW	Cloudy	60	SW	Cloudy = a main street a
Thurs 13	58	NW	Clear	63	NW	Clear
Frid 14	54	NE	Cloudy	60	SE	Cloudy
Sat 15	54	NE	Raining	59	SE	Clear
Sun 16	—	NE	Clear	—	NE	Clear
Mon 17	54	NE	Cloudy	60	SE	Cloudy
Tues 18	50	NE	Cloudy	52	NE	Cloudy
Wed 19	50	NE	Clear	62	NE	Clearing off
Thurs 20	60	NE	Clear	66	NW	Cloudy
Frid 21	58	NW	Clear	62	NW	Clear
Sat 22	56	NW	Clear	66	NW	Clear	aged 5 years. 4 mo. 18 days
Sun 23	—	NW	Clear	—	SW	Clear	inflamation on the brain
Mon 24	66	SW	Cloudy	70	SW	Cloudy	before 12 o'clock mid night
Tues 25	58	NE	Clear	62	NE	Raining	died last night. 10 mins
Wed 26	54	NE	Raining	54	NE	Raining	Harry J. Webber
Thurs 27	50	NE	Raining	52	NE	Raining
Frid 28	56	NE	Trying to clear up	67	NE	Clear
Sat 29	53	NE	Trying to clear	60	E	Clear
Sund 30	—	NW	Clear	—	NW	Clear
Mon 31	56	E	Cloudy	66	S	Clear

On December 23, 1859, their son Harry died.

Amos worked with such prominent blacks as Harriet Tubman (left) and Frederick Douglass.

antislavery rallies. They were also early supporters of Abraham Lincoln. The love they would have given Harry was spent on their fellow blacks.

The country was being torn apart over the issue of slavery and the rights of individual states. Southern states insisted that if they wanted slavery, they should have it. Northern states disagreed. Northerners and Southerners in Congress exchanged insults. A violent mood swept across the country. Many abolitionists felt that political action had failed. Southern states talked about separating from the Union. A newspaper editorial of the time noted: "Our country has two different systems, one resting on slavery, the other on free men. These two systems are moving toward collision."

One evening in October 1860, Amos and Lizzie returned home after attending a political rally in downtown Philadelphia. The election of a new president and the issue of slavery were on everyone's mind.

"I think that Mr. Lincoln is just what this country needs," Lizzie said. Amos did not answer her. He seemed lost in thought.

"What's wrong, Amos?" Lizzie asked. "I can tell that something is bothering you."

"I want to leave Philadelphia," Amos told her.

Lizzie was stunned. She stared at her husband for a while. Then she took his hand and held it. "It's because of Harry, isn't it?" she asked.

Amos nodded his head and tears rolled down his cheeks. "Every time I pass Lebanon Cemetery on my way to work, I think of Harry."

"I miss him so," Lizzie sighed. "If it would help you, I'd be willing to move."

"I've been told that there are lots of jobs in Massachusetts," Amos said. "There are many factories there that need workers."

So Amos and Lizzie sold their home and moved to Massachusetts. Amos found work in the American Steel and Wire Company in Worcester. The move was a big change for the Webbers. Worcester was a small city with fewer than 25,000 inhabitants and a small black population. But it had a black church, and Amos and Lizzie began to put down roots. They both welcomed the new start.

Meanwhile, events were taking place that would further change their lives. In February 1861, representatives of several Southern states assembled in Montgomery, Alabama, and drew up a constitution for a separate country, the Confederate States of America. These states were leaving the Union. President James Buchanan believed that no state had a right to leave the Union but doubted that he had enough power to stop them. His successor, Abraham Lincoln, disagreed. He was determined to preserve the Union—by force if necessary. When Confederate guns opened fire on the United States property of Fort Sumter in the harbor of Charleston, South Carolina, President Lincoln called out the militia. The Civil War had begun.

Although the United States Navy had always

When Confederate guns opened fire on Fort Sumter, President Lincoln called out the militia. The Civil War had begun.

enlisted blacks, the regular army had never admitted them. During the Civil War, for the first time black soldiers were welcomed, although they fought in separate units. Amos Webber enlisted in the Colored Cavalry and attained the rank of sergeant. At the time he enlisted, nearly 150,000 black men were in uniform.

In the army, Amos worked alongside white soldiers and officers. Most of them treated him fairly, but there was always a degree of separation. Whether on or off the military post, a uniform did not protect black soldiers from prejudice. Yet President Lincoln praised them: "With steady eye and well-poised bayonet, they have helped mankind on this great mission."

Amos served with distinction and participated in the defeat of Richmond, Virginia, the capital of the Confederacy. After his discharge from the Union army, one of his officers said to him, "You did what a white man could not do. You knew that the flag under which you fought waved over enslaved millions of your own people. Yet you went to work and fought for that flag."

After nearly four years of bloody fighting, the

Amos Webber enlisted in the Colored Cavalry and attained the rank of sergeant.

blue-clad Union soldiers overcame the gray-clad army of the Confederacy. A shattered South surrendered, and Amos returned to Worcester. He and Lizzie had been apart for too

In the army, Amos worked alongside white soldiers and officers.

long. It was a joyous reunion. They both looked forward to a new life together and made plans for their future. Amos returned to his job at the wire company. Within a year, his salary, coupled with the last of his military pay, allowed the Webbers to purchase a house in Worcester's Second Ward, amid a cluster of other black homes. And Amos and Lizzie bought a piano for the living room.

"I may never be a concert pianist," he told Lizzie, "but music will always be an important part of my life."

Amos and Lizzie remained involved in local affairs. They gave their time to church activities and to social organizations. Amos was a member of several black fraternal societies, and Lizzie was an active member of the Colored Women's Club of Worcester. And Amos continued to share his love of music with his friends.

The Webbers were a proud family. Their lives were shaped by the history of their country, the loss of their son, and their willingness to help others. They were ordinary people who accomplished extraordinary things.

Amos and Lizzie bought a piano for the living room.

The Webber Family Tree

Very few records were kept of slave families, so it is difficult
to trace the roots of African Americans.

We can speculate that in the late 1600s an ancestor of
the Webbers was sold into bondage and brought by ship from
Africa to America, where he was purchased by a Virginia
farmer. Over the generations, his descendants worked as
slaves on Southern plantations.

Around 1785, two slaves married. Eventually, at their
master's death, they were released from bondage through a
provision in his will. They left the South and moved to
Pennsylvania, adopting the surname Webber. (It was common for former slaves to take their master's family name, but
this was not always the case. The surname may have been
that of a friend or have been chosen at random.)

The Webbers lived in Philadelphia, Pennsylvania, and
had a son, Samuel. In 1820, Samuel married Fannie
Johnson. The couple had two sons, Samuel and Amos. The
Webbers moved to Attleborough in Bucks County, outside of
Philadelphia.

Amos Webber, the subject of this story, married Lizzie
Sterling Douglass in 1852. They had a son, Harry. Harry died
in 1859, when he was five years and four months old. Amos
and Lizzie had no other children.

Just before the outbreak of the Civil War, Amos and
Lizzie moved to Worcester, Massachusetts. Lizzie died there
in 1901 and Amos died three years later. Lizzie's tombstone
reads:

Gone but not forgotten

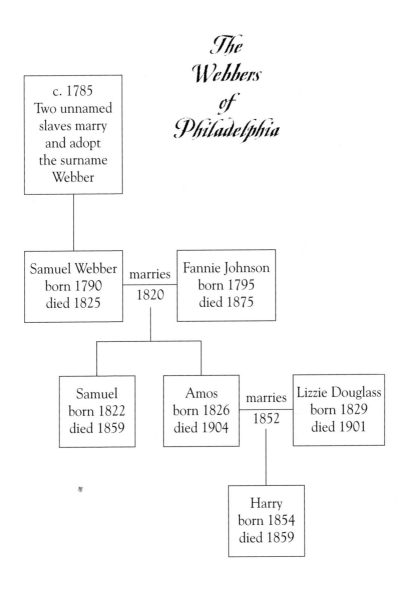

The
Webbers
of
Philadelphia

c. 1785
Two unnamed
slaves marry
and adopt
the surname
Webber

Samuel Webber
born 1790
died 1825

marries
1820

Fannie Johnson
born 1795
died 1875

Samuel
born 1822
died 1859

Amos
born 1826
died 1904

marries
1852

Lizzie Douglass
born 1829
died 1901

Harry
born 1854
died 1859

Places to Visit

To learn more about the history of African Americans, here are some museums and centers of information where you can go:

African American Museum and Library,
5606 San Pablo Avenue, Oakland, CA 94612
Telephone: 510-597-5023
Offers a collection of books, photographs, and artifacts, and a regular schedule of guided tours, lectures, and films.

Afro-American Cultural Center, 401 North Myers
Street, Charlotte, NC 28202
Telephone: 704-374-1565
Housed in a former black church, the Center offers regularly scheduled special events.

Afro-American Heritage Museum, Highway 925
North, Box 316, Waldorf, MD 20601
Telephone: 301-843-0371
Displays artifacts and documents relating to black history.

Afro-American Museum, 701 Arch Street,
Philadelphia, PA
Telephone: 215-574-0380

Contains a collection of paintings, photographs, and artifacts and offers workshops, tours, lectures, and special exhibits.

Black History Resource Center, 638 North Alfred Street, Alexandria, VA 22314
Telephone: 703-838-4356
Contains a collection of photographs and documents and offers lectures, slide presentations, and workshops.

Elfreth's Alley, Old City, Philadelphia

Books to Read

Many good books have been written about African Americans. Here are some titles you might find interesting:

Nonfiction

Bial, Raymond. *The Underground Railroad.* Boston: Houghton Mifflin, 1995.

Marston, Hope I. *Isaac Johnson: From Slave to Stonecutter.* New York: Dutton, 1995.

Medearis, Angela. *Come This Far to Freedom: A History of African Americans.* New York: Atheneum, 1993.

Stanley, Leotha. *Be a Friend: The Story of African American Music in Song, Words & Pictures.* Middleton, WI: Zino Press, 1995.

Yates, Elizabeth. *Amos Fortune, Free Man.* New York: Dutton, 1967.

Fiction

Carter, Donna R. *Music in the Family.* Chicago: Lindsey Publishing, 1996.

Johnson, Dolores. *Now Let Me Fly: The Story of a Slave Family.* New York: Simon & Schuster, 1993.

Knight, James E. *Seventh & Walnut, Life in Colonial Philadelphia.* Mahwah, NJ: Troll Communications, 1995.

McKissick, Patricia. *Freedom Is More Than a Word: The Diary of Clotee, a Slave Girl, Richmond, Virginia, 1859.* New York: Scholastic, 1997.

Rosen, Michael J. *A School for Pompey Walker.* San Diego: Harcourt Brace, 1995.

Weinberg, Larry. *Ghost Hotel.* Mahwah, NJ: Troll Communications, 1994.

Index

Page numbers for illustrations are in **boldface**.

About the Author

J. Loeper was born in Ashland, Pennsylvania. He has been a teacher, counselor, and school administrator. He has both taught and studied in Europe.

Mr. Loeper has contributed articles and poems to newspapers, journals, and national magazines. He is the author of more than a dozen books for young readers, all dealing with American history, and an active member of several historical societies. The *Chicago Sun* called him the "young reader's expert on Americana."

Mr. Loeper is also an exhibiting artist and has illustrated one of the books he authored. He and his wife divide their time between Connecticut and Florida.